I Know I Can!
Do The Laundry

ANTHEA DAVIDSON-JARRETT
Illustrated by
Aldana Penayo
Published by EDUCATE THE GLOBE,
London, UK, 2020.

ISBN: 978-1-913804-02-2

Copyright © 2020 Educate The Globe Limited. All rights reserved. No part of this book is to be reprinted, copied or stored in retrieval systems of any type, except by written permission from the author. Part of this book may, however, be used only in reference to support related documents or subjects.

I know I can do it!

Please can I help?

I want to do it all by myself!

Please can I try?

Can you show me how?

I'm not too small;

I am ready right now!

We've come back from holiday.

It was so much fun.

We climbed mountains and scuba dived.

Enjoyment for everyone!

But now I'm in the kitchen;

so many clothes to wash!

Socks and pants and vests and tops

and shirts and. . . oh gosh!

When my friends and I

were chasing butterflies

I fell over a rock.

Stained my skirt; then I cried.

When we were eating dinner

after the theatre show,

I spilled sauce all over

my dress and my elbows!

My trainers got all wet one day;

it was so very funny!

My mummy was upset

as they cost a lot of money.

When we got home

Sana played a trick on me.

We started ramping in the garden

now my blouse is filthy!

Mummy shouts "Come here!

Let's sort out all these clothes."

I need to teach myself

how this washing thing goes.

First we must put

everything in a different pile.

Whites and darks and colours.

Shoh! This will take a while!

Make sure that all the fabrics like silk, cotton and jeans are put to spin separately in the washing machine.

We also need to make sure the temperature is right.

We check the labels on the clothes so they won't shrink overnight.

The machine dries our clothes

so all we have to do

is iron and fold them

then put them in our rooms.

Mummy will do the ironing

I will fold my clothes.

I think I will be good at it

so off we go!

Spread my tops on the bed

so the front is laying down.

Bring the sleeves in

then fold like Sana's doing now.

Socks are so easy

when you've had a few tries.

Do like I'm doing;

you'll be a master in no time!

Trousers are simple too;

just look at how we do!

Fold them at the waist

then again times two!

So much to remember

when you're wash and folding clothes!

Now I'll make a salad

with some beans and tomatoes.

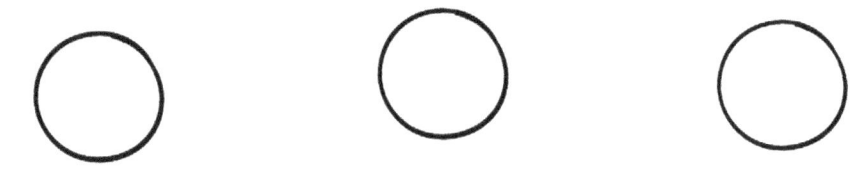

www.ingramcontent.com/pod-product-compliance
Lightning Source LLC
Chambersburg PA
CBHW041245240426
43670CB00027B/2991